Falling in Fun Again

Doris Jasinek and Pamela Bell Ryan
Illustrated by Caroline Price

CompCare® Publishers
Minneapolis, Minnesota

Jasinek, Doris.
    Falling in fun again/Doris Jasinek, Pamela Bell Ryan:
 illustrated by Caroline Price.

    p. cm.
  ISBN 0-89638-227-3
  1. Love — Humor   2. Interpersonal relations — Humor
  I. Ryan, Pamela Bell.   II. Title.
  HQ801.J37 1991
  306.7 — dc20   90-45791
                                 CIP

Illustrations by Caroline Price
Cover and interior design by MacLean & Tuminelly
Jane Thomas Noland, contributing editor

Inquiries, orders, and catalog requests should be addressed to
CompCare Publishers
2415 Annapolis Lane
Minneapolis, Minnesota 55441
Call toll free 800/328-3330
Minnesota residents, 612/559-4800

  6   5   4   3   2   1
 95   94   93   92   91   90

To Joy and Beth and Sally,
who have always known what fun is.

fun n. 1. A source of enjoyment, amusement or pleasure 2. Enjoyment; amusement 3. Playful and often noisy activity. —intr. v. funned, funning, funs. To behave playfully; joke

The American Heritage Dictionary,
Second College Edition

One morning you wake up to the sound of the same old alarm, put on the same old coffee pot, stare at the same old sleepy faces. One is your own—in the mirror. The other belongs to the person you're closest to in all the world.

As you greet each other in the same old way, you realize that this day promises to be a lot like yesterday—and that tomorrow probably will be a lot like today.

You know that everything's all right. Your relationship is comfortable. Your life is pleasant. You're very grateful for that.

Still, you say to yourself, "Maybe we need to fall in fun again."

Maybe you even say it to each other.

Do you sometimes long for the times gone by, the old songs, the old crowd—that gang of friends who really knew how to have fun! Do you miss the young "me" or the romantic "us"?

Don't wait until the mortgage is paid, the basement is clean, the kids are grown, or you've lost weight to enjoy your life.

Rock the routine. Put some hum in your humdrum.

Start now to...

...fall in fun again!

Are You Having Any Fun?

When was the last time you laughed until you were weak?

Or sat on the grass together, looking up at the sky and picking out faces and animals in the clouds? Or hiked to a hilltop to view something new? Or happened upon a concert in the park—and stopped to listen?

When was the last time you got excited about something and set out to learn as much as you could about it?

Or surprised him (or her) with a hug? Or paused to watch a very young child—yours or someone else's—in the incredible process of exploring the world?

When was the last time you could honestly say you were having fun?

Funcheck

Try this funcheck:

___ Do you look for—and find—humor?

___ Do you often applaud or cheer?

___ Do you smile a lot—or grin or giggle?

___ Do you often laugh out loud?

___ Are you glad to be with the one you're with?

___ Do you have a song in your heart?

___ ...a lilt in your voice?

___ ...a spring in your step?

Happiness and fun often overlap!

Funmeter

Where are you on this funmeter?

I am having...

Even if you place yourself at the the top of the scale, you can boost your funmeter score higher still—along with your spirits. It requires awareness and practice. But there's no ceiling on fun!

The time of my life!

A blast!

A kick!

A ball!

A natural high

Some mildly enjoyable moments

A faint sparkle of fun now and then

Mostly lacklustre days (and nights)

The blahs

The blues

Funlight

Everyone starts out life with a funlight. Some continue to let it beam out brightly. Some let it dim with time and responsibilities.

Look for your funlight if you've misplaced it. Carry it with you wherever you go. Let it shine on your relationships with life, with others, and with yourself.

They're Fun!

Some twosomes are happy in their work and spontaneous in their play. They overcome adversity rapidly. If they don't get the table by the window, dinner isn't ruined. And their walk goes on in spite of the rain.

Sometimes the traffic IS heavy, the airline loses luggage, or the food is terrible.

But these two think ahead. They imagine themselves — later — telling their sympathetic friends about these misadventures and annoyances.

They're fun to listen to — fun to be with.

Spin your tales with laughter.

Shed funlight on your recollections.

Shine it on your partner-and-fellow-adventurer too.

Keep your parasols down. Let the fun shine in.

Step by Step to Fun

What can you do to add fun to your life and your relationship?

1. Get rid of your funblocks—whatever keeps you from having fun.

2. Practice funstarters—allow yourself to be open to fun.

3. Become a funseeker—discover your own, individual fun. Define—honestly—what's fun for YOU.

4. Then discover the joys of funsharing and...

...fall in fun again!

Get Rid of Your Funblocks

Finding an appreciation for life is difficult if it's being eclipsed by a funblock. The following beliefs and attitudes create common funblocks.

Funblock No. 1: The "I must act my age" fundowner

Those who refuse to take part in an activity because they believe they've "outgrown such foolishness" are suffering from a true fundowner. They say such things as, "She should know better than to try to be a majorette at her age!" They refuse to join the three-legged race or the egg toss at the company picnic. They choose to stand still and watch other couples walking on the beach, even when THEY could use the exercise—and the handholding.

To overcome the act-your-age fundowner, be a participant in all your relationships, young and old. And remember, roller skates, bicycles, slides, and swings come in all sizes.

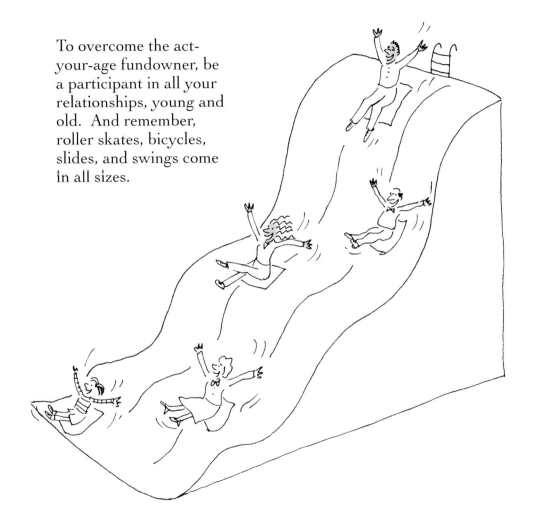

Funblock No. 2: The "I must always be who I'm expected to be" funscreen

You live behind a funscreen if you feel the need to "fit" your established roles at all times: the stern and in-control father; the gotta-make-it-big-in-the-professional-world woman; the high-risking executive; the Supermom or Supermate. Do you worry a lot about what to say, what to wear, what to serve, whom to spend your time with? If you try constantly to measure up to others' (and your own) expectations of yourself, you will probably screen out your fun.

Stop protecting your super-responsible image behind a funscreen! Give in to spontaneity. Have a get-together and dress up or dress down—or out of style. But know that you never have to disguise yourself in order to have good, clean, classic fun! People who respect your capabilities will appreciate your lighter side too.

Funblock No. 3: The "I don't deserve to have fun" funfoil

You'll foil even the possibility of fun if you view fun only as a reward for goodness or accomplishment. Anyone whose self-esteem is shaky—or who comes from a family in which nobody had much fun—is likely to feel "undeserving" of fun.

Foil this funfoil by affirming repeatedly to yourself, "I don't have to EARN fun" (you don't!) and "I DESERVE to have fun" (you do!).

Funblock No. 4: The "I've got a million excuses" funburner

You may recognize this funblock. It's the funburner habit—the chronic, crippling tendency to make excuses for not having fun. Do you automatically turn down suggestions or invitations? Are you the one who backs out of fun at the last minute? Do you rationalize away your fun with funburner statements like these?

"We can't get a babysitter."

"It costs too much."

"I'm too tired."

"It's more trouble than it's worth."

"The weather's too damp (or cold or hot or windy)."

To avoid the funblock of constantly burning your own fun (and other people's too), reschedule some fun—and then follow through. Expect the best (and accept the worst). You may be happily surprised. Remind yourself: excuses will always be there; today will not.

Funblock No. 5: Fun-a-phobia

You may have the most serious funblock of all—fear of fun, or fun-a-phobia. You may believe that if you loosen up to allow fun into your life, somehow you'll be out of control.

The only remedy for fun-a-phobia is letting a little fun happen, in a small way at first. Then you can see for yourself: the consequences of honest fun— fun that harms no one—are not fearful, but life-enhancing.

Practice Funstarters

Be ready for fun, open to it, willing to LET FUN HAPPEN.
To allow yourself be open to fun, you may need to:

Lighten your mood. Let go of tension, whirling thoughts,
assignments, problems. "Letting go" is a prerequisite to
fun. Stop and listen to peaceful music or nature
sounds—birdsongs or meadow noises or the wash of waves
on a shore. Relax and give yourself permission to have fun.

Lighten your load.
Let go of your too-tight schedule. Unburden yourself, at least temporarily, of your daily routines. Break free, and open up to the possibility of fun.

Lighten your outlook.
Savor the excitement of an upcoming event. Do you remember when you were a child and anticipation was half the fun? Try to recall and recreate that open-to-fun feeling.

REALLY lighten up! Let yourself be carried away by fun!

Find Your Own Fun

Questions for Funseekers

Your fun doesn't have to be the same as your parents',
your peers', or Pee Wee Herman's. Tailor-fit your fun to
your own lifestyle. The following questions can help you
find YOUR fun.

Do you enjoy being the...

—student

—performer

—player

—giver

—receiver

—follower

—speaker

—leader

—listener

—teacher

—audience

—spectator?

It's your own fun. Be as many of these as you like.

Is your fun quiet? Or humming with hubbub?

What's the pace of your fun? Meandering? Marching?
Sprinting? Sitting (feet up on the ottoman)?

Do you like your fun
outdoors? Water fun?
Land fun? Fun where
they meet (on the
shoreline)?

Or indoors? In a simple
setting? In a grand
setting?

Is your fun comfortable oldness? Familiarity? Returning to a place you like? Seeing old friends?

Is your fun newness? Excitement, discovery, new places, new views, new skills? Testing yourself in new situations?

Does your fun involve a lot of people? Or few people?

Is your fun anticipating? Or recollecting?

Rank Your Fun

Rank the following from 1 to 10, from most to not-so-much fun.

Vehicles for Fun

Point out your favorites.

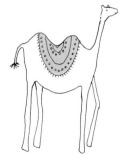

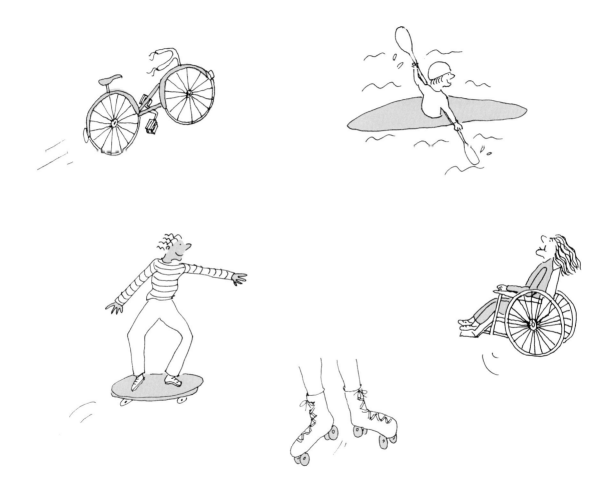

Finding Your Funspot

The following brief exercise can help you find your funspot—the place you'd like to be most in all the world. Pretend you're there, and write a "having wonderful time" postcard to yourself from that place. If your "having fun on a trip" self were writing to your everyday, at-home self, what would you say?

Fill in the blanks:

Dear Me,

Having wonderful time, doing _____,

seeing _____, reading _____, just

relaxing on _____ with _____.

Love, Me

Funsharing

Now, having explored your personal ideas of fun,
share them with your mate, soulmate, spouse.

Compare what the two of you have discovered as your individual ways to have fun.

Examples:

Her idea of fun:

1. the opera
2. skiing
3. the kids' soccer games
4. going out to dinner
5. long walks on the beach

His idea of fun:

1. a baseball game
2. skiing
3. the kids' soccer games
4. reading at home in front of the fire
5. short walks in the woods

Their idea of fun:

1. skiing
2. the kids' soccer games
3. medium-sized walks in a beachside grove

Which of the other's "discovered" fun are you willing to try?

Which activities can be compromised or modified slightly so you both can enjoy them? Which will probably remain your individual pursuits of fun?

You'll have more fun together if you have fun apart—if you're not exclusive funpals, counting solely on each other for fun.

Alternating Fun

If your kinds of fun don't always match
and you want to be together, try alternating
fun—the things *you* love to do and *he/she*
merely likes with the things *she/he* loves to
do and you are less enthusiastic about.

If you're planners, budget your fun.
Balance *your* days or evenings or weekends
of fun with *her/his*. But always allow for
more of the kind of fun you both enjoy.

If spontaneity is important to you, don't
overplan. Just be sure you're sensitive to the
other's likes—don't overload the scale (or the
calendar) with your own individual fun.

Honest Fun

If there is something you want to do,
be honest. Make your wishes known.
See how he (or she) feels about it. And, if
it's the kind of fun you agree on, share it.

If you don't agree to share it, explain
that you'll do it by yourself—without
resentment, happily, because you CAN
enjoy your separate fun.

You, as an individual, are responsible for
generating your own feelings of fun.

Fun for Grown-ups

Adult relationships don't have to be predictable or unexciting.

Have the courage to change your appearance, your routine, or your tone of voice.

If you have only one important thing going for you in your relationship, let it be an attitude of fun. Without it, there is no laughter, no polka, no reason to get up in the morning.

Commit Random Acts of Novelty

Leave notes in her lunch, on his mirror, on her pillow, in the car.

Have breakfast for dinner, breakfast in bed, or breakfast at the beach.

Wear crazy pajamas.

Take the scenic route instead of the freeway.

Plant something tropical.

Try an exotic recipe—together.

Monogamous doesn't have to be monotonous!

Funning Interference

Sometimes it's hardest to have fun with someone you live with. Do you allow yourself to be irritated by lights left on, the out-of-balance checkbook, or the pile of dirty socks strewn around the floor? Such irritations may be funning interference in your life!

Let fun start with an attitude of gratitude—focused on what a great friend she is, or how much he loves you and the kids.

After all, what's most important—love, friendship, or dirty socks?

Let perspective be your backdrop for fun.

Protect Your Funshine

Avoid the cloudy ones who can puddle up your fun—
especially the fun you enjoy as a twosome. Everyone
knows people who are valued friends or relatives, but are
grumps, lumps, pessimists, or complainers—in other words,
non-fun.

They make excuses for not having fun:

"I don't have anything to wear."

"I have nowhere to go and no money to get there."

"I've never done that before."

"Today is Thursday."

"My wife (husband) doesn't even know how to have fun."

"I'm too old."

"I won't fit in."

"I'm too young."

"They won't miss me if I don't go."

"It will be too crowded."

"What will people think?"

You can react in many ways to their attitudes of non-fun.

You can leave them under their clouds. You can like
them in spite of themselves. You can complain and
commiserate along with them. You can try—gently—
to pry them out from under their gloom into the fun.
You may be surprised that these people have funstreaks,
after all. If they won't budge, don't allow them to cloud
your own fun.

Life is never cloudless.
But we can have fun in spite of the clouds.

Don't go through life with shades on.

Wear funglasses.

They're Fun

They're fun. They laugh at themselves and at their own foibles. They've made light of situations that others find hard to handle.

Whether we're invited for a formal dinner or a neighborly tuna-and-macaroni hot dish, we feel at home in their home. They let us help. We laugh along with them.

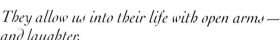

They allow us into their life with open arms — and laughter.

They're fun.

Fun is open.

Fun welcomes.

Fun risks being a little outspoken.

Fun supports. (It's never humor at the other's expense.)

Fun is catching!

Fun Can Be a Trip

Your postcards to friends at home are scribbled testimonials to shared fun on holidays.

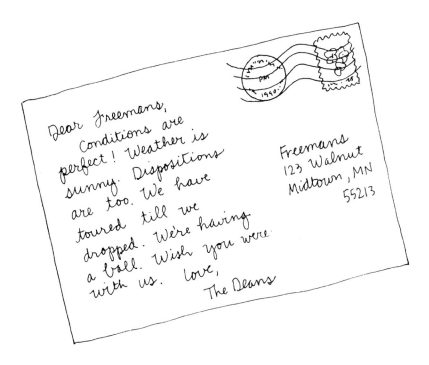

Dear Freemans,
Conditions are perfect! Weather is sunny. Dispositions are too. We have toured till we dropped. We're having a ball. Wish you were with us. Love,
The Deans

Freemans
123 Walnut
Midtown, MN
55213

Dear Johnsons,

The air is clean and the views are magnificent! We've hiking 12 miles a day now and will reach a lodge tomorrow (where we'll mail this). Can't wait for a shower and REAL food! We can see why the brochures label these trails "Recapture the Romance" and "Follow the Fun." There's some of each! You two should try this!

Gary and Carole

Johnsons
446 Birch Trail
Blue Lake, IN
62611

Dear Jenny and Mark,

In spite of detours, car trouble, Montezuma's revenge, we've made it to our destination each night. This trip has been a disaster but funny! We've laughed ourselves silly. Can't wait to show you dozens of photos and laugh some more. See you soon — we hope.

Mary & Jay

The Whites
722 Lake Ave.
Palmer, CA
90046

Fun Can Be a Gift

A time-out-for-fun when it's been a busy day.

A surprise vacation just to say "I love you."

A swing on a swing to reawaken the child-inside.

A puppy (but only if you've agreed on it beforehand).

A hug when that's all you have to give.

Realize Your Funabilities

Fun need not be saved for holidays and weekends.
Let fun into your life together at all times. Funability is
a way of seeing and discovering what's fun. It's also the
ability to laugh at yourselves—gently, lovingly, openly.

Develop your funabilities.

Enterprising Fun

Imagination is part of fun. Develop your fun-imagination.
Do something out of the ordinary.

Walk up the middle of a rocky stream (not a swift one)
in your tennis shoes.

Take a night off at a bed-and-breakfast inn. It may be three
or thirty miles from home, but you'll feel as though it's
three-hundred!

Build an unusual snowperson.

Write a play for the gang or the family to produce—lights,
costumes, and all.

Cook Italian, speak Italian, hug Italian—just for one night,
just for fun.

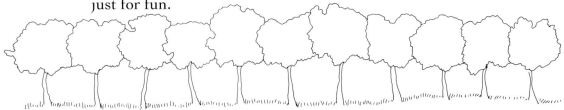

Surprising Fun

Surprises are part of fun!

Coming upon an abandoned house at the end of a gravel road during a drive in the country.

Putting together an instant picnic. Pick up some fast food and eat it together on a warm hillside in the spring or in a pocket park in the city.

Sharing the discovery of a giant trillium beside a spongy log in the woods.

Meeting a new couple in your building with interests (and senses of humor) that coincide with yours.

Trying a restaurant from a different culture.

We Have Fun

We're quite a pair! People are surprised when we tell them how long we've been together.

We do our best to keep our lives upbeat and interesting. When schedules get hectic, we don't see each other enough. But there's always a secure feeling that a quick squeeze or a smile will bring us back in touch.

We argue sometimes. But we laugh about it afterwards.

Our life together is a kaleidoscope of experiences — some sad, most happy. And we always leave time — and room — for fun.

Fun-raisers

Whisper. Blow a kiss. Present a bouquet. Leave a card propped up on the hall table. Talk a walk (hold hands). Meet for lunch.

Celebrate an anniversary of the day...

> she got her degree
> we moved to this house
> he made a hole-in-one
> he passed his state boards.

Create a new anniversary...

> "I'm Glad We're Still Together" Day
> "I Balanced the Checkbook" Day
> "I Love You Even Though You Didn't Get the Promotion" Day
> "We're Going to Have a Baby" Day
> "We Walked Five Miles" Day.

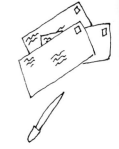

We Work Together — for Fun

We work together. And we make our jobs fun. Playfulness never lessens our production or diminishes our professionalism. In fact, banter gets us through high-pressure deadlines.

In our family business we celebrate everything from birthdays to Groundhog Day — with cards, balloons, home-grown roses, and computer-printout banners.

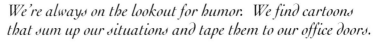

We're always on the lookout for humor. We find cartoons that sum up our situations and tape them to our office doors.

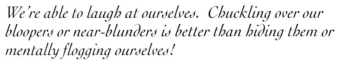

We're able to laugh at ourselves. Chuckling over our bloopers or near-blunders is better than hiding them or mentally flogging ourselves!

Lightheartedness lightens our work load. We share our work — and our on-the-job fun! We're lucky.

Take a Funbreak Together

People in serious pursuits especially need funbreaks:

> detectives and traffic officers,
> sergeants and bishops,
> chefs and liontamers,
> ecologists and pathologists,
> CEOs and BMOCs and Ph.D.s,
> you and me.

There will always be moments when it's okay to joke around. Moments to act as young as you feel. And moments, even in the most formal or solemn times, when smiles are appropriate.

No matter how intensely you approach life, take a funbreak together and...

...fall in fun again!

Fun for Two

Rent a tandem.

Play a duet.

Have a little tug-of-war.

Play tennis or ping-pong.

Well, yes—tango.

Fun-damentals

Laughing at each other's laughter

Recollecting past fun in peaceful moments

Appreciating two-ness

Small talk

Pillow talk

Not having to talk

Fun Together

Fun together is:

F — Freeing yourself from whatever keeps you from having fun

U — Unstressing your life, to allow yourself to be open to fun

N — Negotiating your fun together

Fun can't be arbitrated, but it can be negotiated.

For some, fun is light.

For some, fun is laughter.

For some, fun is music.

For some, fun is a featherbed.

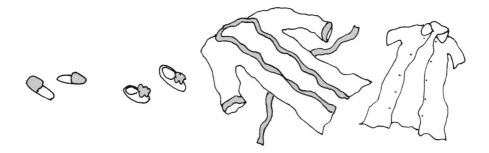

Fifty Years of Fun

We've been together fifty years and we're still having fun.

Our hearts are full of laughter, even though:

I can't hear so well. He can't see so well.

We walk now. No more marathons.

We go out in a rowboat. No more kayaking.

We sing in the chorus. Not solo.

I drive at night. He drives in daylight.

We study for pleasure. No pressure for grades.

Changes? Yes.

Less fun? No.

Our hearts are full of laughter.

Sparks of Fun

Whether the relationship is two years old or twenty or fifty or more, rekindling sparks of fun will add to your ongoing glow of happiness together.

Get in touch with the vitality within you that wants to laugh, learn, love—and have fun.

If you feel like dancing, dance.

If you feel like wearing silly hats, wear them.

If you feel like singing, sing. (Harmonize!)

If you feel like laughing, don't be afraid to laugh out loud.

And if you're having a good time, tell each other.

It's never too late to...

...fall in fun again!

About the Authors

Doris Jasinek, now director of Grace Children's Center in Des Moines, Washington, is an education specialist who has spent twenty years as a teacher, administrator, camp director, consultant, and lecturer. For fourteen years she was director of Bethlehem Community Preschool in Encinitas, California. She studied at University of California in San Diego, San Diego State University, and University of London. She has two grown children and three grandchildren.

Pamela Bell Ryan, a graduate of San Diego State University, is completing a master's degree in post-secondary education. She is director of St. Andrew's Preschool and Intergenerational Program in Encinitas. She and her husband, Jim, and their four children live in Leucadia, California.

Both authors spend much of their professional time with children, who are, after all, the best teachers of fun!